Purpose Poems

By Michael P. Earney

Copyright Michael P. Earney 2022
All Rights Reserved.

No part of this book may be reproduced, stored in a retrieval system, or transmitted by any means, electronic, mechanical, photocopying, recording, or otherwise, without written permission from the author.

ISBN-13: 978-1-956581-20-1 PB

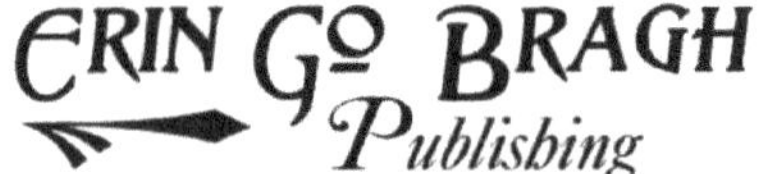

Canyon Lake, TX
www.ErinGoBraghPublishing.com

Introduction

Each of the poems in this collection was written with a purpose in mind. My A-to-Z series of books started with, The A-to-Z book of Birds, it wasn't until the next in the series, The A-to-Z book of Wildflowers that I started with a poem. I don't recall what prompted me to do that, but since then, each of the books in the series starts with a poem, and the second edition of Birds was given not one poem, but two. Not all of the poems appear in specific books, but most are inspired in some way, by the writing and publishing of books.

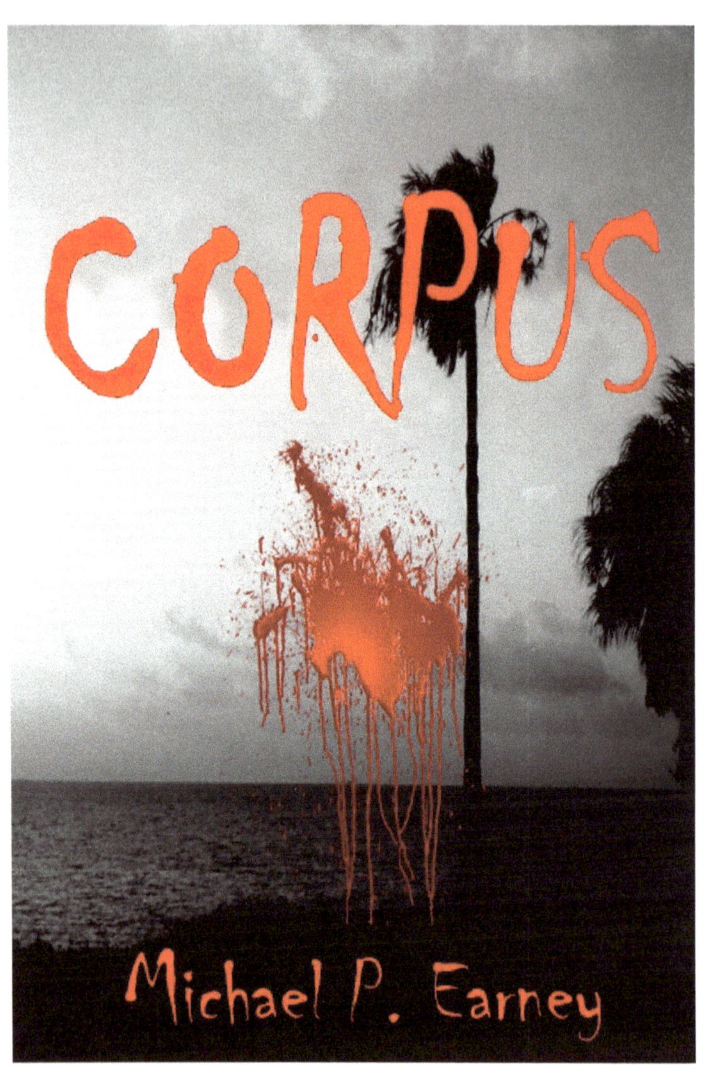
CORPUS
Michael P. Earney

Bookworm

Oh Wow! Look at you, you wrote a book!
I just can't guess how long that took.

Did you sit there, day after day
writing, writing, writing away?

A murder mystery? That's bound to sell.
There's a billion out there but, what the hell.

It's an achievement and you should be proud.
Go out and tout it clear and loud.

Build a website, a Facebook page, you can't just stop.
With good reviews the Amazon list you'll top.

Well, yes, first you'll need an editor
so's your English don't read too poor.

Layout, cover design, these you'll need to find.
An ISBN and copyright also come to mind

Publishers you'll have to ring,
expect a callback, only if you're Stephen King.

But wait, there are publishers who'll name a price.
There's lots of those, they're just like lice.

And once your book has gone to press,
their interest will go from less, to less.

Now you can get your book at wholesale,
buy a bunch and sell yourself, at retail.

Those, that is, you don't give away
or the others you may just mislay.

There are Book fairs, and Festivals galore
though travel, hotels, and eating out
may cost you more.

Now, don't forget that retail tax
there are penalties for being lax.

Bookstores may take them on consignment
a percentage of such sales go to pay their rent.

Schools and libraries, now there's a thought
though that will mostly come to naught.

Still, you can look for fame and fortune.
With luck, you just may gain a portion.

And, if after all, you're still a pauper,
at least you're now a published author.

~ Michael P. Earney
2022

Bookworm Continued

Now that your first book's finally out
Another book's about to sprout!

You write and write and write some more,
It's easier than it was before.

You know what to do and how it all works,
You write stuff to go with your artworks.

You've cultivated lists, know who to call,
Know which shows to attend this Fall.

Figuring the many books you have to sell,
It looks as though you're doing well.

Upsales will come, customers come back,
You're a published author, you got the knack!

With each published book you reaffirm,
That you, yourself, are a bookworm.

~ Kathleen J. Shields
Approved by the author - 2022

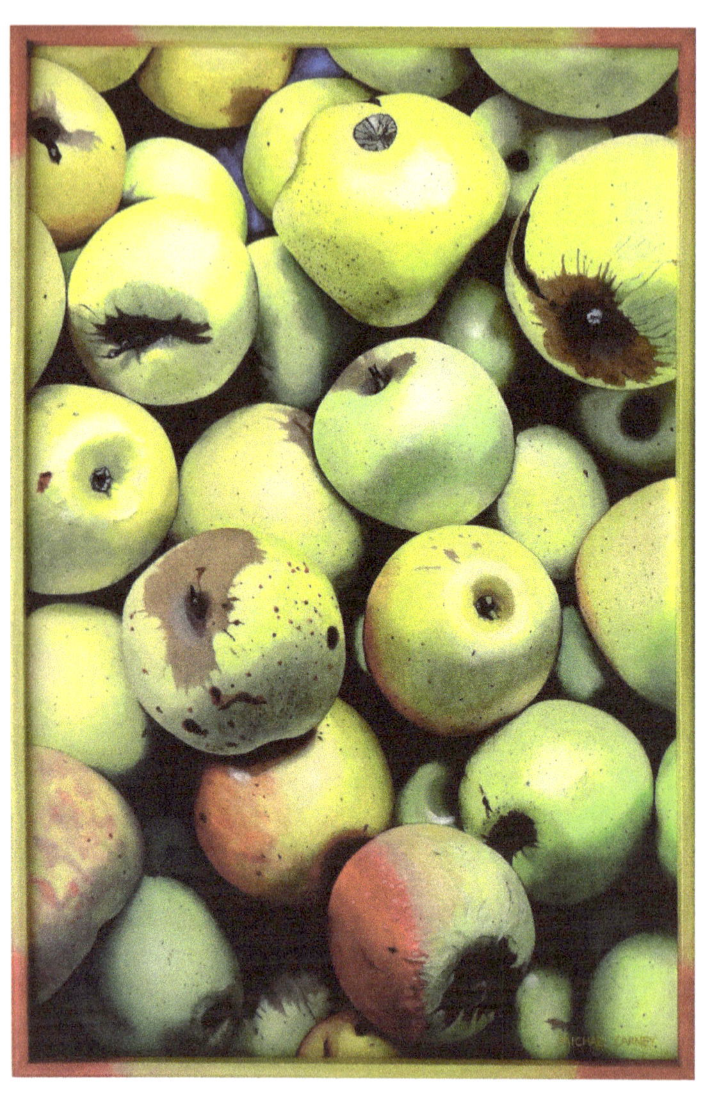

Golden Delicious
from the Mexican Produce Collection

Words of Purpose

An apple a day keeps the doctor away
at least, that's what the old folks say
Pride goes before a fall,
A stitch in time saves nine, and all.

In times when people couldn't read or write
such pithy sayings kept them bright
the Book of Proverbs was compiled to help one out
keeping us on the right path is what it's about.

It's chock-a-block with words of wisdom
though some strike me as slightly dumb.

In the end, it really serves its purpose,
to remind us, life is quite a circus.

Speaking of Platitudes:

So, you're up the creek without a paddle,
did you lose the bubble?
Did you walk under a ladder?

didn't keep your fingers crossed
or knock on wood?
Did a black cat cross your path?

That should have raised a red flag.
Perhaps you bought a lemon or,
a pig in a poke.

Maybe you were trying to make
a silk purse out of a pig's ear.

You didn't count your chickens
before they were hatched, did you?
Or put the cart before the horse?

Anyway, you're the scapegoat
and got sent to Coventry.

Certainly, you got the short end of the stick.
But hold your horses!
You may have bitten off
more than you could chew
and therein lies the rub.

You are not whistling in the dark.
You could drum up something good
if you keep your powder dry
and don't mix apples and oranges.

Now, if you can't take the heat,
stay out of the kitchen but,
if you are not at the end of your rope
and willing to put something on the table,
the coast is clear.

There are more ways than one to skin a cat, my friend.

Grab the bull by the horns,
leave no stone unturned then,
by the skin of your teeth
you could pull something out of the bag.

Things could be coming up roses,
you might find yourself living in clover.

Don't give up the ghost,
don't throw in the towel.

Rome wasn't built in a day
and remember,
it ain't over till the fat lady sings!

Break a leg!

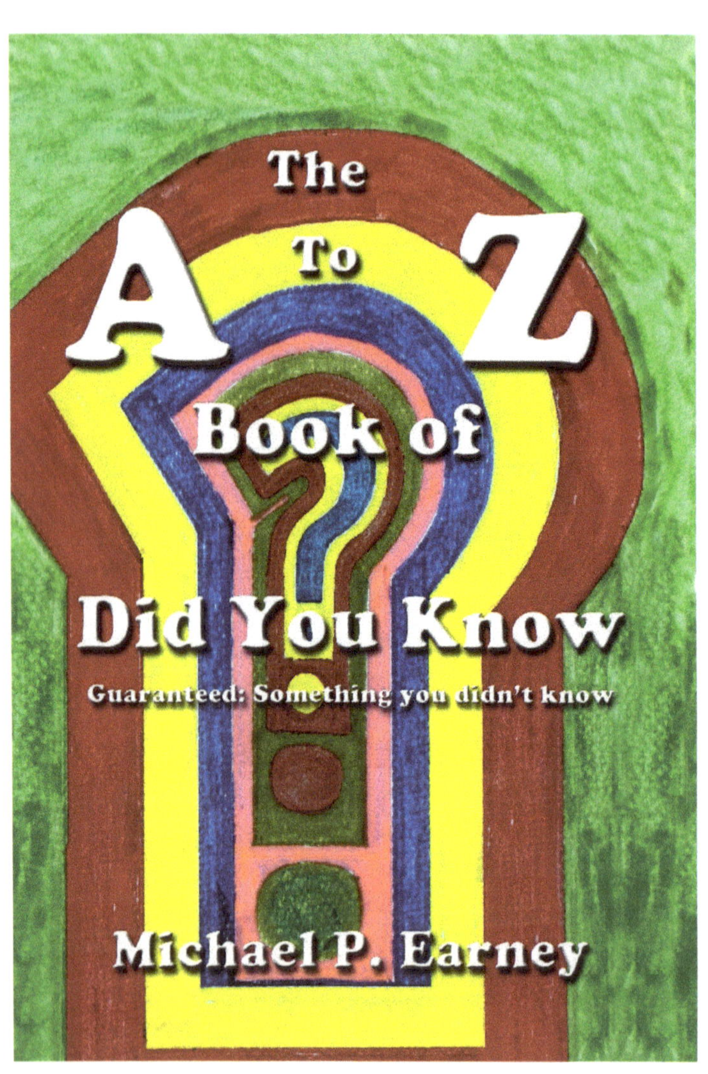
The
A
To
Z
Book of
Did You Know
Guaranteed: Something you didn't know
Michael P. Earney

If I Knew

If I knew all there was to know
would I be wise, would I have more dough?
Or would confusion rule my days?
as I chose between the yeas and nays
of what is right and what is wrong
make sage decisions all day long.

If I were a judge of every case
the losing side I'd have to face.

My every word I'd have to weigh
that this must go but that can stay.
Contentious views would fill the air
can being right as well be fair?

When certitude gives way to doubt
it might be wisest to step out
or wisest yet, let it be said,
just empty out my aching head.

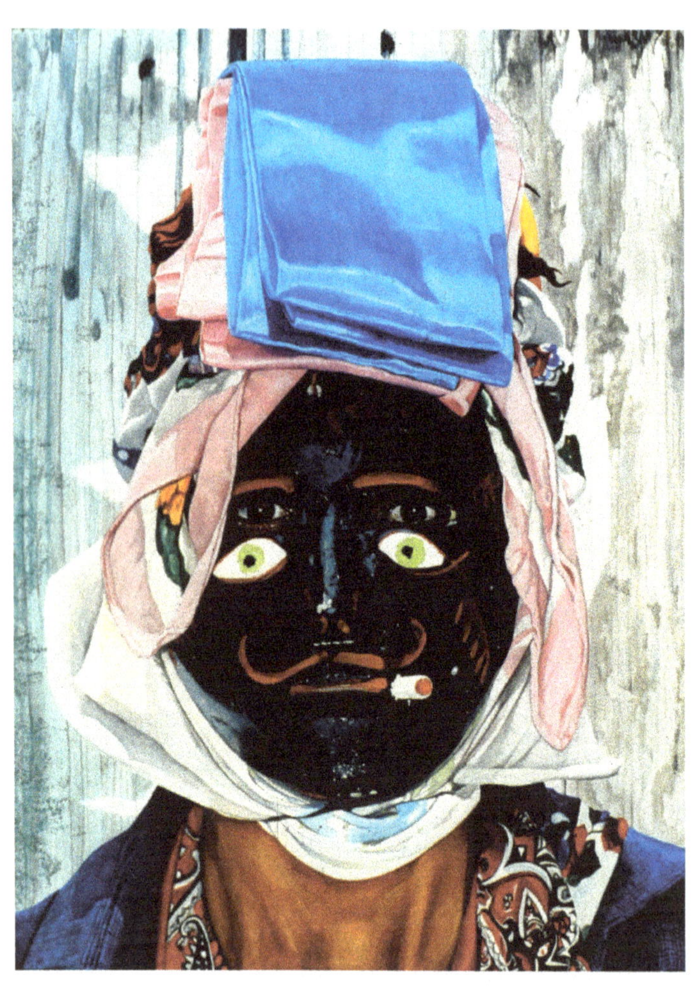

Artwork from *Magic Faces / Caras Magicas* Book

To Be

There is a face behind the face
that we present to all the world to see.
To hide that face is no disgrace,
it's just the way it has to be
we have to keep up our facade,
to go along and not be proud
to humbly show all due regard,
and never stand out from the crowd.

But if you think that you can take the heat
that you'll prevail what e'er the fight
then there's no reason to retreat.
Just say, I'm different, it's my right!

Assert yourself both night and day
and staunchly hold your line!
Just forge ahead in your own way
I guarantee you'll do just fine.

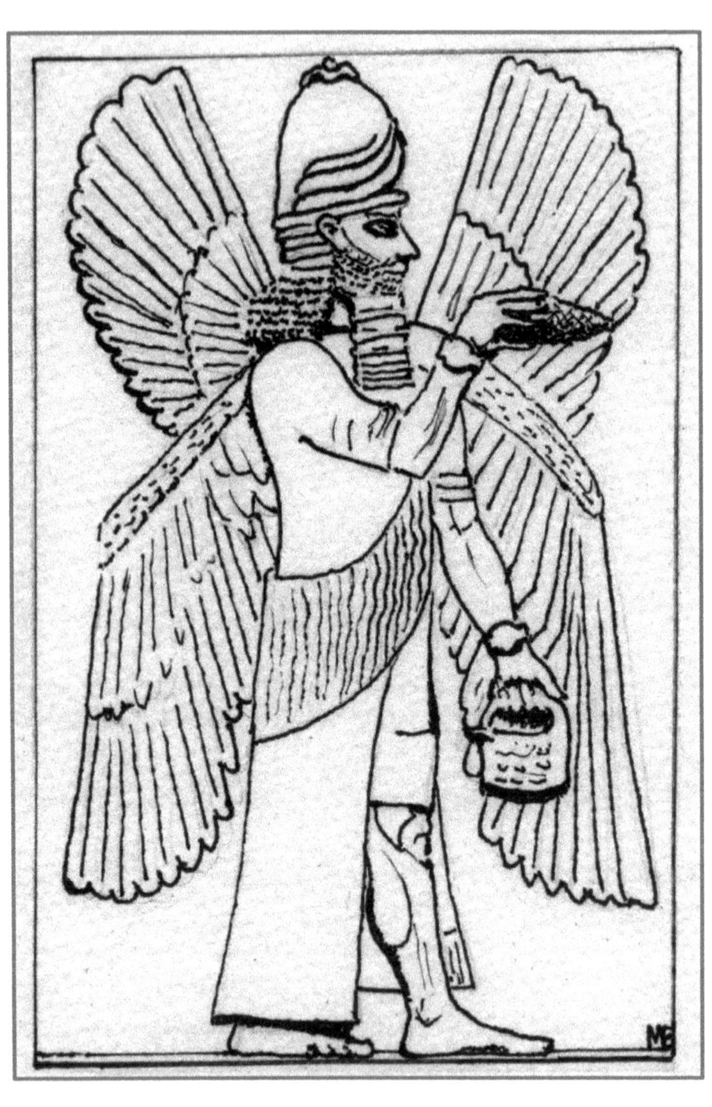

Artwork from the sketchpad of Michael Earney

Entered in a joke competition. It didn't win.

From Sumer with humor

The first ever joke, at least, the one that is known,
was told by an ancient Babylon.
Yes, you guessed right, it tells of a fart.
And from that early auspicious start,
the genre has grown from fart to fart.
After centuries of building on such great wit,
we now see jokes become part of English Lit.

if you had in mind a similar rhyming word
I'll say it for you, you were thinking of turd.
But, please, jokes don't all have to be crude
there are plenty of clean ones equally rude.

With double entendres and words left unsaid,
it's clear we the audience are just being fed,
since it's up to us to fill in the blanks,
these are often the times a joke fizzles and tanks.
And if the laugh this time happens to be on you,
trust that, at some point, the jokester will get his due.

So, then everyone gets to laugh in the end
though, not too hard or your pants will rend.
Go ahead, giggle and snicker and have a good time
Then I'll have achieved what I hoped with this rhyme.
If I can't elicit at least a tee-hee,
then it will be clear that the laugh is on me.

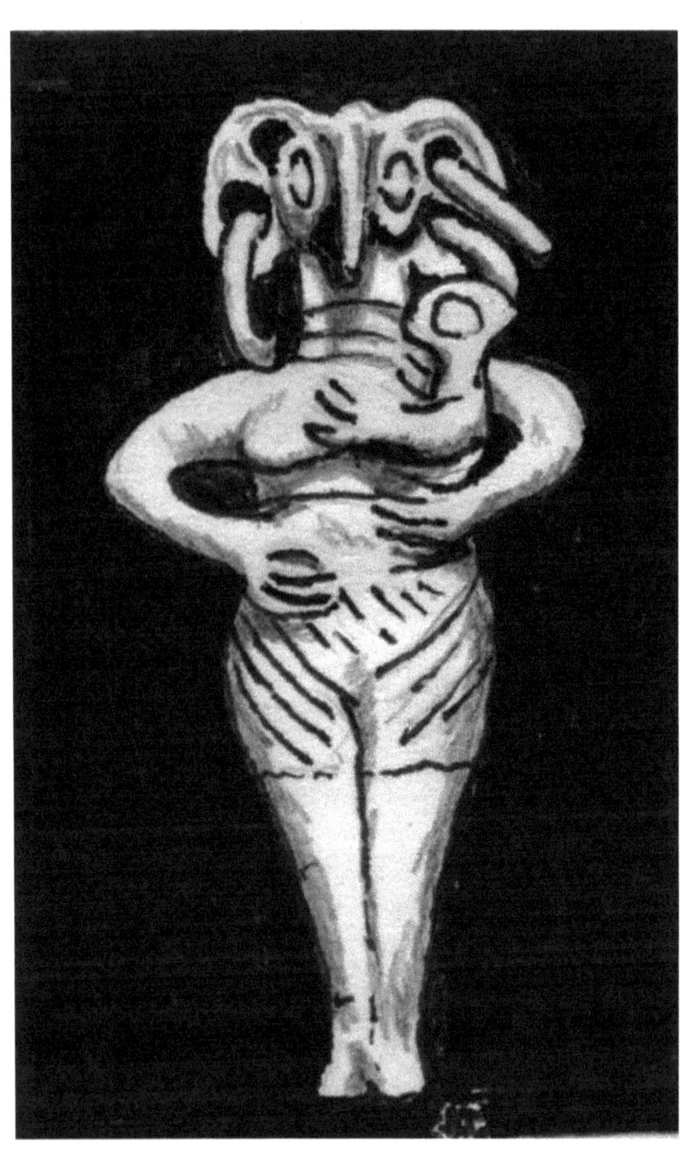

Cretan Owl Goddess

Holy Cow!

Goddesses have had their day
it's over now, they've gone away.
'Tis true most places in the world
in others though, their spell has held.

Goddesses of which you've never heard,
unless you are a Goddess nerd,
continue all their heavenly tasks.
And what are they, a youngster asks?
To protect, to heal, provide so many things,
a cornucopia of gifts she brings.

Goddesses helped folk throughout the day
when in doubt, they showed the way.
How to weave and how to write,
how to love, and how to fight.
And when a person's time had had its run
they led the way to kingdom come.

Each one had her special duty
as Heavenly mother or, as nature's beauty.
Metis, Astarte, and Venus are ones I knew,
though Isis, Athena, and Nut should get their due.
Those goddesses who once ruled the world
were mistresses of all that they beheld.

Myths and legends now are all that's left
their stories show how truly we're bereft.
Were those deities that once guided nations
but figments of Mankind's imagination?
Or do people, who to goddesses still turn,
hold some truths that we should learn?

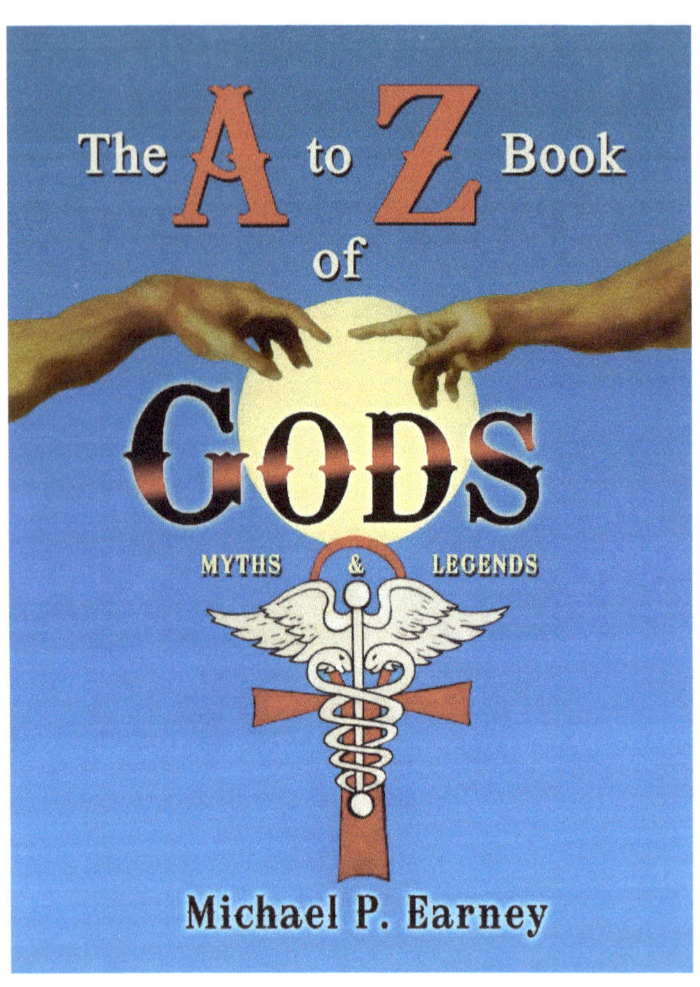
The A to Z Book
of
GODS
MYTHS & LEGENDS
Michael P. Earney

Ye Gods!

Do the gods of Olympus still look down from on high?
Does the kitchen god still preside when we fry?
They are all around us, one for this, one for that
for the doorway, for the hearth, even one for the cat.

A Lord of the Thunder, a Lord of the Rain
Is that a god flying? No, it's only a crane.
Still, they do come along in a number of guises
so, you need to be ready for any surprises.

With so many gods to adore and placate
that one simple slip-up could seal your fate.
You must have faith and say all of your prayers
That way, in the end, you may go "upstairs"

And, if at last, you get to the "Heavenly Gate"
Have your answers all ready, St. Peter can't wait
There are plenty of souls being placed on the scales,
those that spoke wrongly, that sound is their wails
as they head for the fire and brimstone below,
The place where, believe me, you don't want to go.

There are plenty of choices,
so, that's the good news
just hope that your loved ones
go along with your views.

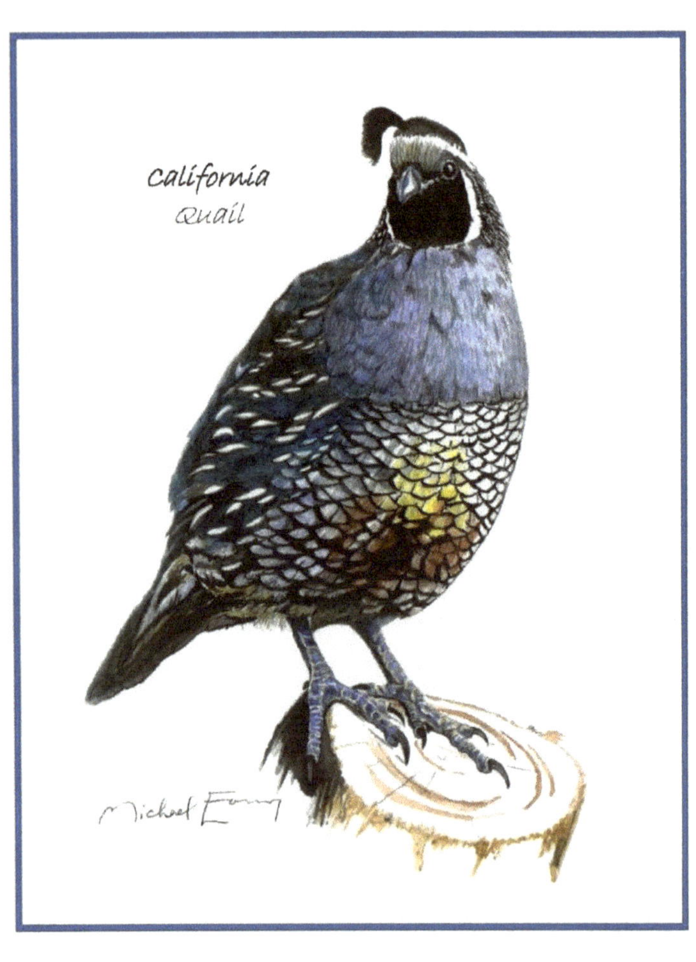

Bonus Artwork from *The A to Z Book of Birds*
An A to Z for young bird lovers.

What the Flock

A kettle of Hawks circling high in the sky
looks down on a gaggle of Geese
as a paddling of ducks passes by,
near a sedge of Cranes, that we hope will increase,
with that ballet of Swans, pray they'll never cease.
For that murmuration of Starlings,
we've nothing to fear,
like a quarrel of sparrows, they'll always be here.
An unkindness of Ravens, a building of Rooks,
a murder of Crows
they're all rather dull,
as a flamboyance of Flamingos easily shows.

Still, even a puddling of Mallards
outshines that dark three.
As a bright charm of Goldfinches
sing-along from a tree,
across the wide lake, and its asylum of Loons,
an exaltation of Larks joins in with their tunes.

Then, a deceit of Lapwings makes a cast of Jays scold,
that's a tiding to Magpies, best not be too bold.
Should a banditry of Chickadees
give a bad name to fowls,
the judging we'll leave to the wisdom of Owls.

Now, for those among you who think birds only flock,
I'm sure that the foregone has been quite a shock.
Still, there are only so many could say that I fail
If we come to the end with a covey of Quail.

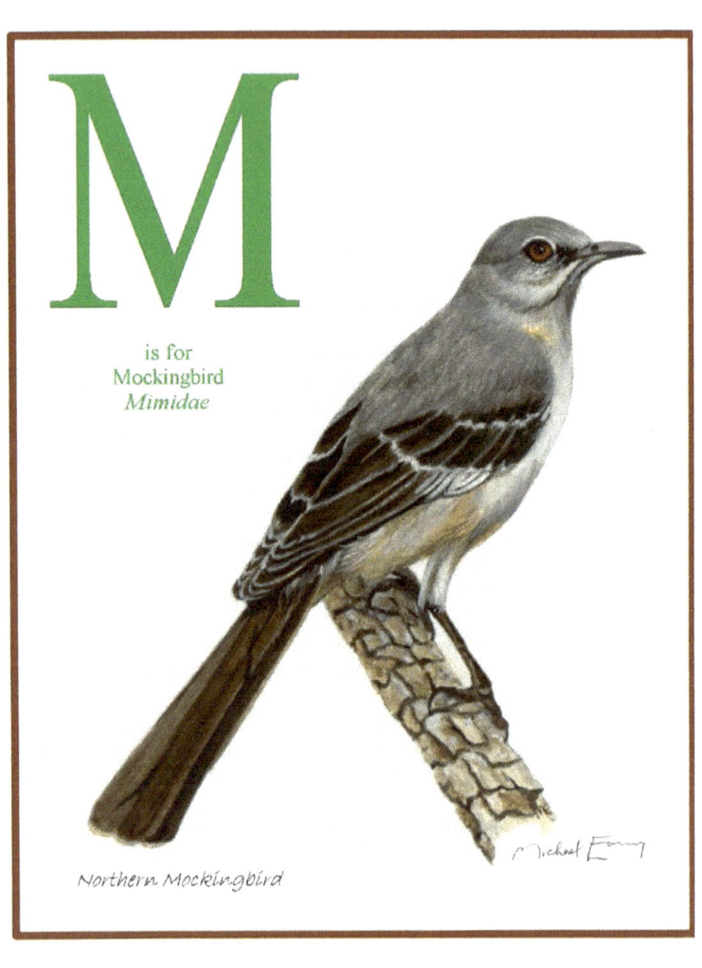

Artwork from *The A to Z Book of Birds*
An A to Z for young bird lovers.

For the Birds

Trills, coos, tweets, and chatters greet the dawn
birds in the sky, birds in the trees, birds on the lawn.
The sound of birdsong brightens every day
though less and less, it's sad to say
The Dodo and that pigeon, gone,
and countless others too.

No one's to blame, but me and you.
Another is your kitty cat,
birds disappear, while cats grow fat.
herbicides and pesticides
contaminate the food birds eat,
windmills, windows, cars, and planes,
their ranks deplete.

It's true, the Whooping Crane's back from the brink,
but other species see their numbers shrink.
The Condor that once soared on high,
it seems as though its end is nigh.
The Heron at the water's edge,
the wise Owl calling in the night,
the Eagle and the Hummingbird,
their future isn't looking bright.

Now, you and I can turn this thing around,
raise up your voice and make a sound.
Tell those who great decisions make,
to "Save the Birds!"
Our very way of life's at stake.

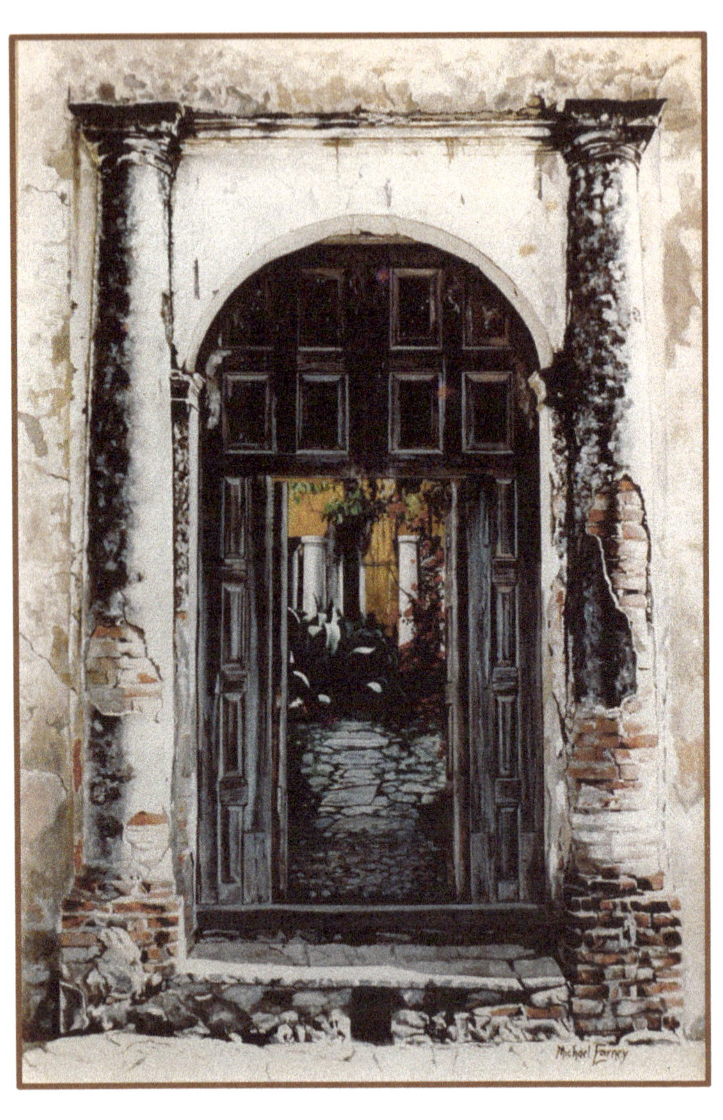

Artwork from *Entradas, Mexican Doors*

Doors

There are entrances and exits,
this way in, that way out
swinging doors and those that slide,
still others, like a round-about you ride
and some that just go up and down.

Take care it doesn't catch your gown.
you can be happy when you get in
or glad that you got out.

Now, entrances that have a guard,
for those you'll need a special card,
that use fingerprints, or facial recognition,
as the only way, you'll gain admission.

You and I both know this is your address,
So there's no reason you should be denied access.
No pass? Lost your keys? Just come in with me
or, like Santa, you can use the chimney.

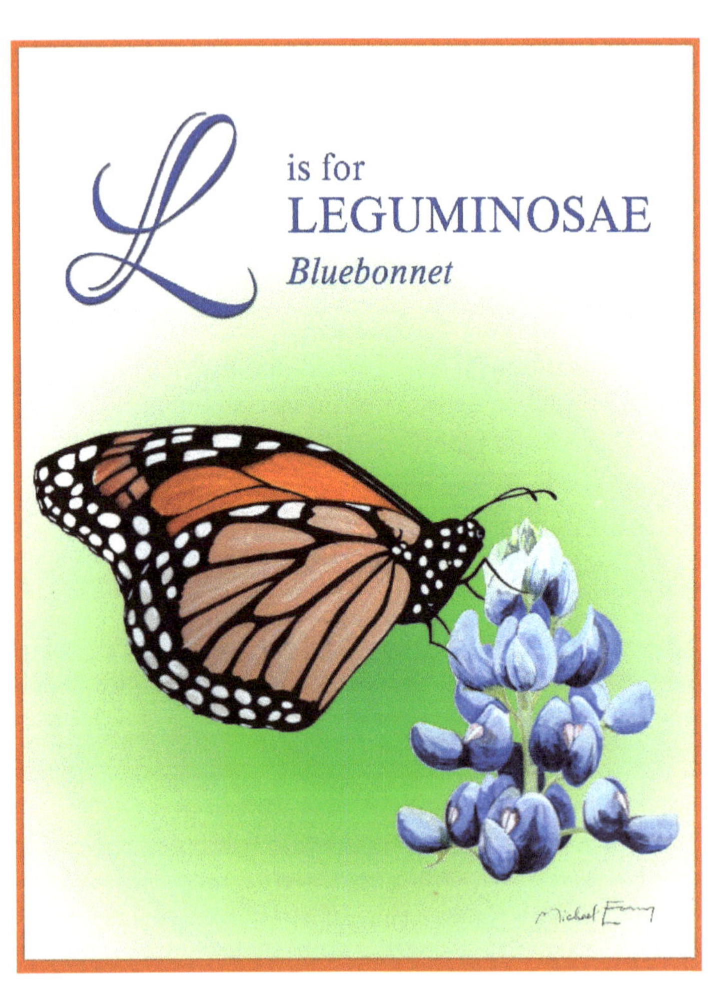

Artwork from *The A to Z Book of Wildflowers*

Plants

If plants could talk, they'd never stop,
they have so much to tell!

They know the story of the earth and sky,
They know the birds, they know the bees,
They know the butterfly!

There are plants that walk, there are plants that climb,
There are plants that live beneath the waves
Then plants that float across the seas,
And even plants that fly!

Plants heal the sick
And give us all our daily bread
They house us, clothe us, keep us warm
And cook the food that they provide
Since first we came into this world
They've given us the air we breathe
in simple truth, without the plants,
Mankind could not survive!

Their beauty is beyond compare
A multitude of colors, shapes, and sizes,
So many fragrant scents that fill the air!

With humble gratitude for all they share
let us as one our voices raise
Forevermore to sing their praise.

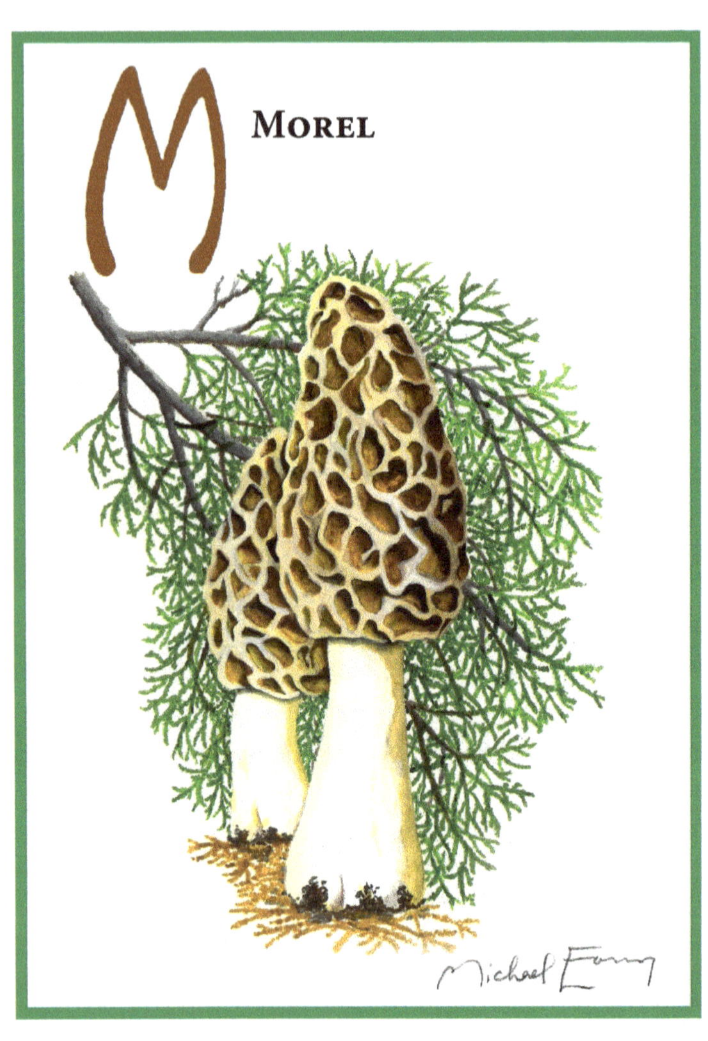

Artwork from *The A to Z Book of Mushrooms, Which to Enjoy and Which to Avoid*

For Mushrooms

The words fungi and mushroom
don't roll off the tongue
They're smelly, they're nasty,
they grow mostly on dung!

At least, that's the perception some people hold.
To eat a wild mushroom, you have to be bold
Or stupid, or crazy, those people would say.
It grew in the woods? You should throw it away!

If only they knew what you and I know,
They'd be out there seeking to find where they grow.

Once hooked on the mushroom, you never go back.
For breakfast, lunch, dinner, or just a quick snack
They're delicious, medicinal, and magical too!
In their hundreds, their thousands, or only a few.

You seek under ledges, wade grass to the knees,
You jump over fences and start to climb trees.

Although there are many you may never see,
Do get to know those that it's best to let be.

Their names, now familiar, roll off the tongue
Shaggy Mane, Chanterelle —
and those growing on dung.

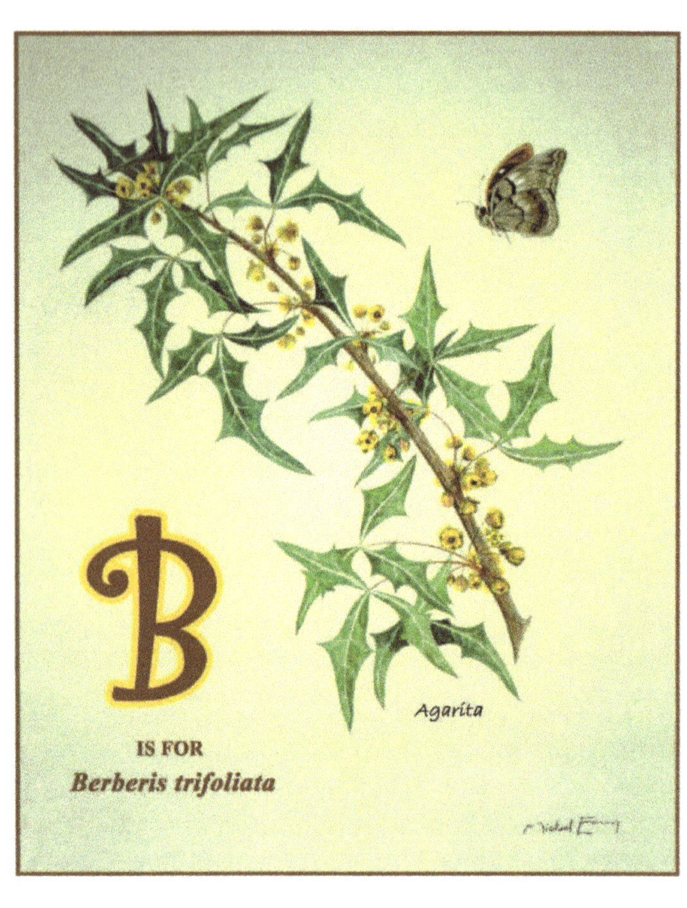

Artwork from *The A to Z Book of Weeds and Other Useful Plants*

Weeds

Weeds, those pesky plants we throw away,
we slash, we burn, dig up and spray.
What good are they? You may well ask.
To answer this is no small task.

Herein, you'll find a small selection,
to point you in the right direction.
If you get sick, are taken ill,
you have a sprain, or take a spill,
it's to the weeds for help you first should turn.

There, remedies abound, you'll quickly learn.
Take roots, leaves, stalks, flowers, fruits, and seeds.
The things you need are in the weeds.

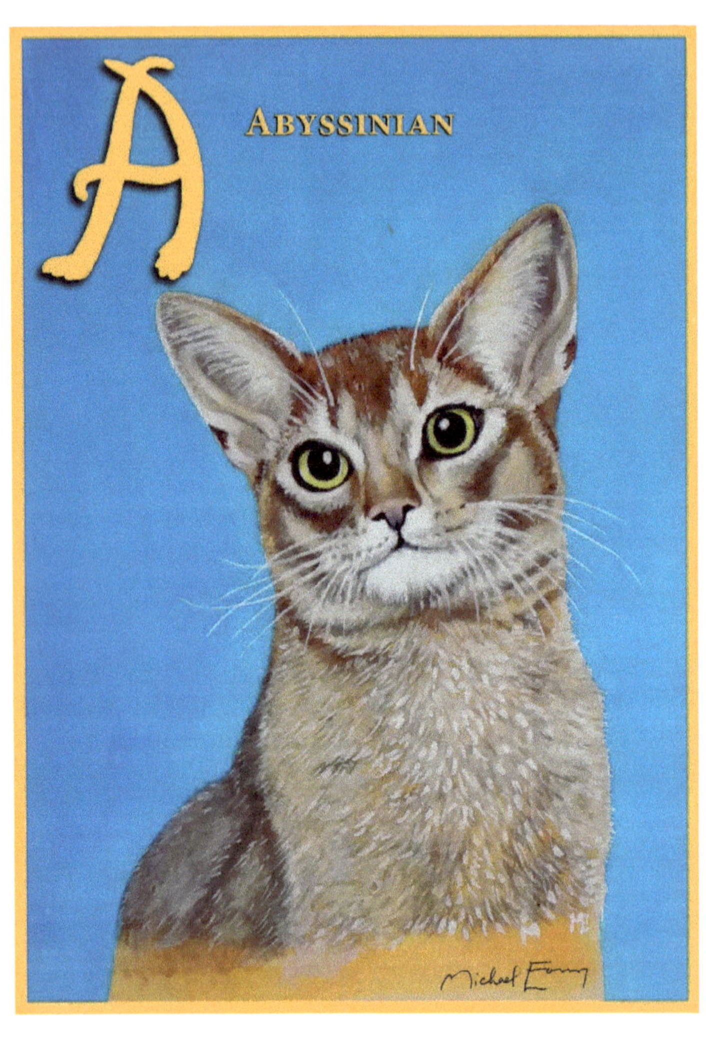

Artwork from *The A to Z Book of Cats, Wild and Domestic*

The Cat's Meow

There are lions and tigers and lynx
there's Siamese and Burmese and a cat named Sphynx
there's cute and cuddly with soft, tiny paws
then there's fierce and savage with sharp, deadly claws
just as pumas and leopards can tear you apart
a Kurilian bobtail plucks the strings of your heart.

while it's lovely to hear those soft, soothing purrs
it's best to remember, they are all carnivores
from panthers that threaten the ranchers' herds
to your little kitty-endangering birds.

While bobcats are shot as protection for sheep
the millions of birds killed raises scarcely a peep.

Of course, your house cat is precious to you
but all of the big cats could use some love too
Cheetahs, the fastest mammals on land,
like all of the wild cats, they sure need a hand.

It's essential we keep their homes free and wide
in order to show them, we're taking their side.

Cats, gone from the wild, would truly be sad
leaving just cats, domestic, as all that we had.

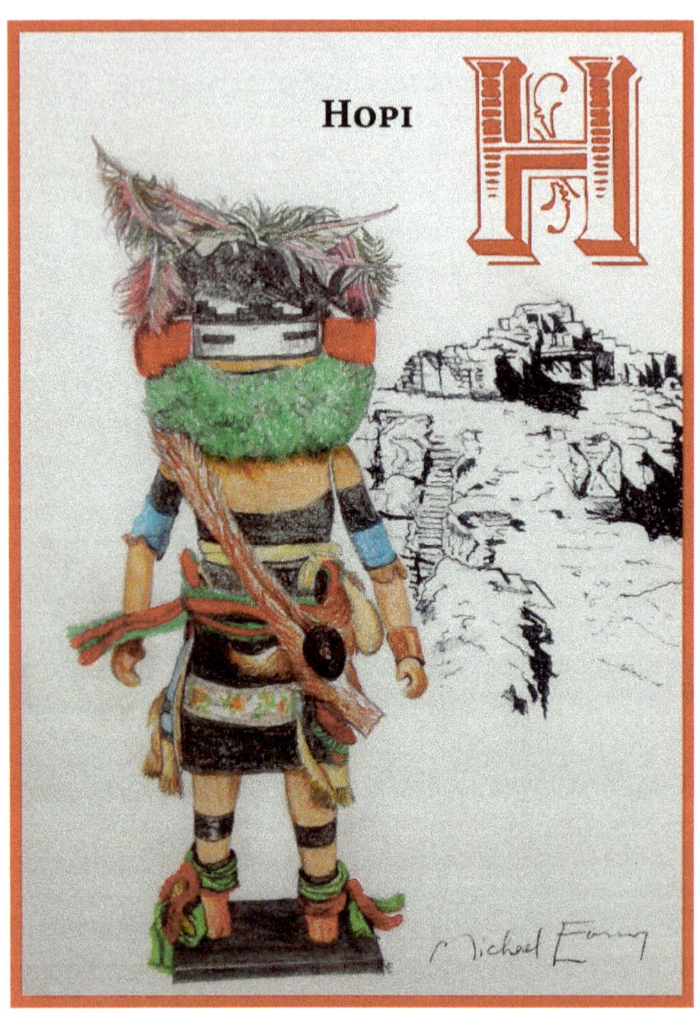

Artwork from *The A to Z Book of Turtle Island, Land of the Native American*

This Land

In 14 hundred and 92 Columbus sailed the ocean blue.
And what did he find for me and you?

America! This great land of the free
named for Americo Vespucci.
He was the one who called, 'Land Ho!'
Raising cheers, from those on the deck below.

However, long before Columbus came,
America had another name.
For the People waiting on the shore
Turtle Island was the name it bore.

Yet, before these folk could have their say,
their lives and ways were swept away
Disease and warfare thinned their ranks.

For which, the settlers gave God thanks.
They then went on to build a nation.

and, though seldom in the best location,
some tribes did receive a reservation,
(Where you can go when on vacation).

Accepting those that have a different way of life
has put an end to all that bitter, mindless strife.

Still, to some, it must sound really rather odd,
to say that we're one people under God

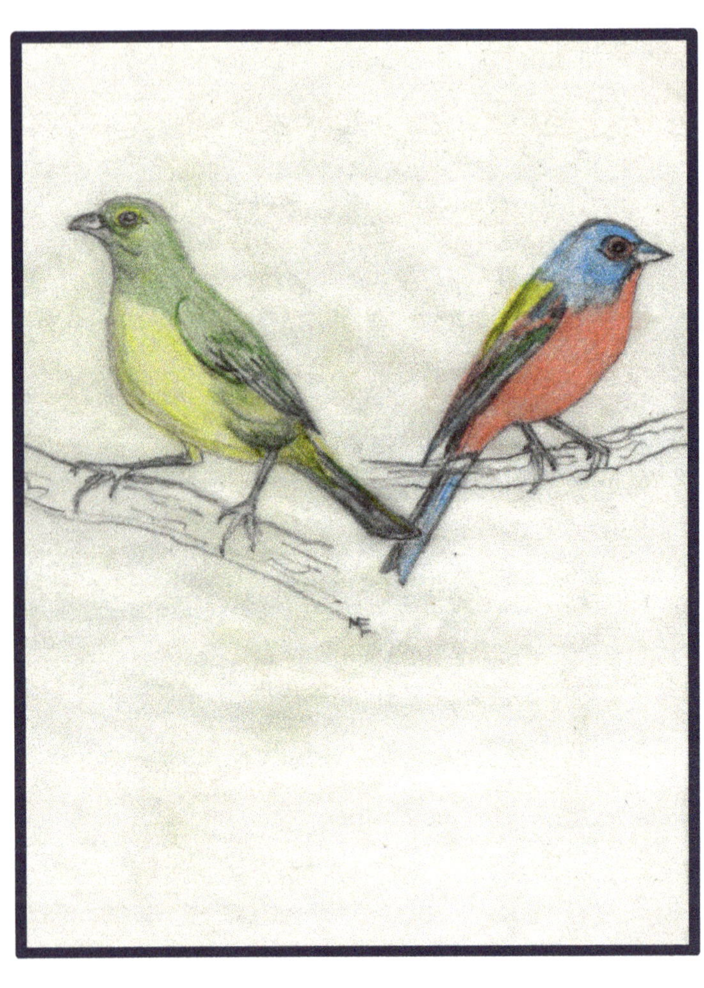

Artwork from the sketchpad of Michael Earney

Timmy the Painted Bunting

Pretty little Mrs. Painted Bunting
for a home, she was a hunting
(Low shrubs or trees close to the ground,
where she is not too easily found)

She had flown in from far, far away,
so as to arrive on this warm Spring Day.
(Nearly one thousand miles, you know.
That's a very long way to go.)

Soon she picked a shrub that was the very best
and there she made her baby buntings' nest
(A Bunting's nest is like a cup,
a lovely place for growing up)

In that small nest, she lay three eggs
one was Charlotte's, one was Tim's,
and one was Greg's.
(Five is what a Bunting lays at most,
but Mrs. Bunting didn't want to boast)

Then Mrs. Cowbird came and laid another
so that Mrs. Bunting should be its mother.
(Cowbirds are such awful pests,
they lay their eggs in other's nests.)

That cowbird chick grew large and moved around
pushing little Timmy to the ground
(Cowbirds hatch out sooner than the others,
and grow much faster than their stepbrothers,)

The neighbor girl who lived nearby
saw that Timmy now might never fly
(Those who spend their time outside,
see things we miss by staying inside.)

She took that baby to the family farm,
there Timmy grew and came to no more harm.
(A bunting usually lives five years and then….
but, with luck, they might live for ten.)

Timmy recovered strong and hale,
So, this becomes a happy tale.
(Cowbirds often throw the mother's eggs
out of the nest,
Those Cowbirds, as I said, can be a pest!)

Having once lived in Port Aransas, Tx,
when I learned that a plan to establish a crude oil storage and shipping facility on the ship channel there was to be presented to the city council,
I wrote the following to the editor of the local paper.

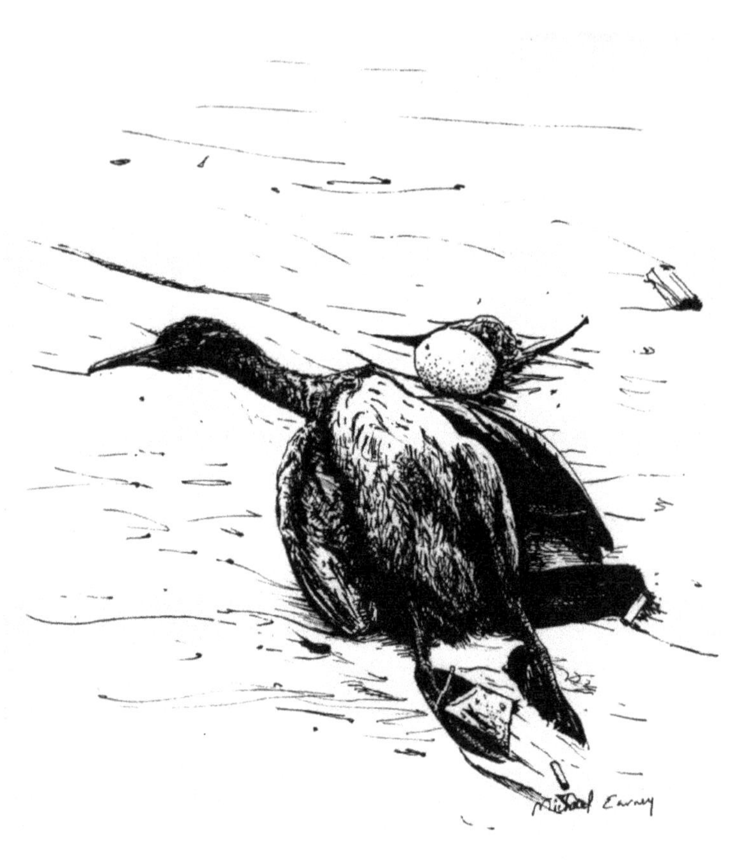

Artwork from the sketchpad of Michael Earney

Crude

I come to you on this auspicious day
not to tell you what it is we'll take away.

Oh no! The news I'll do my best to sugar coat
it's about this, eh, kind of little boat.

You see, we need a place to load some crude.
At your front door, would that be rude?

Since there's no room in our neighborhood
we thought your pristine landscape would be good.

Don't worry about the noise and grime
you'll get used to it in time.

Now, we guarantee all the work we do
and if it fails, well then, just sue.

There'll be no leaks, of this we're sure
unless a hurricane should come ashore,
then someone else will clean up the mess
and we'll just move on, I guess.

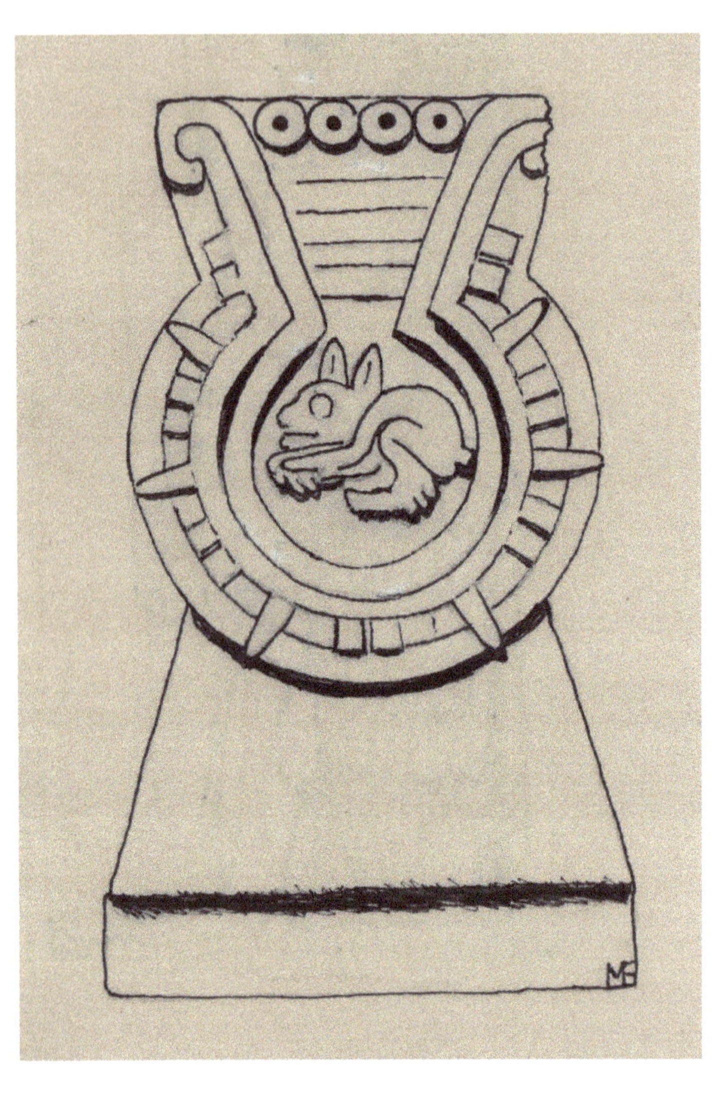

Rabbit in the Moon,
Mixtec stela from Tlaxiaco, Oaxaca, Mx

Moonlight

There's a partial eclipse of the moon tonight
if you asked, partial? Yes, that's right.

A partial eclipse seems like no big deal
but this one's special and that's for real
as 98% of the moon will disappear
and it will take its time to reappear
5 hundred 80 years have come and gone
since there was another quiet this long
true, the eclipse of 2018 was 12 minutes
longer than this will be
but this one's partial, as you will see.

It's called a 'Blood Moon' for its reddish hue,
a 'Beaver Moon' or, 'Micro Moon', will also do.
Now, if you can't stay up that late
you won't have very long to wait,
in 2022 there's to be not one, but two,
in May and November is when they're due.

Though, if tonight's is the kind to which you're partial
your 'stay up' strength you'll have to marshal.

About the Author

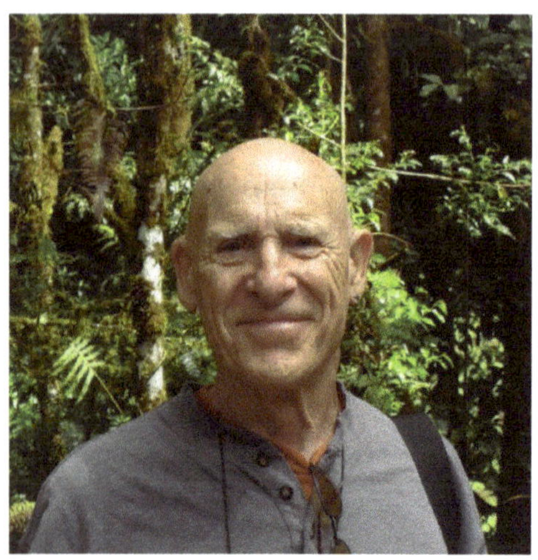

Michael P. Earney is a fine arts painter who grew up in England. His writer's voice reflects curiosity and passion for the world of nature. His text is instructive yet playful. The illustrations are executed with grace and fine detail. Earney is in his element as artist, writer, educator, and naturalist. To learn more about this author's books and various achievements please visit his websites.

Contact Mr. Earney: themichaelearney@yahoo.com

Websites: www.MichaelEarney.com

Publisher:
www.ErinGoBraghPublishing.com/authors/mearney

Collect All of the A to Z Books!

The A to Z Book of Birds
The A to Z Book of Cats
The A to Z Book of Did You Know
The A to Z Book of Gods
The A to Z Book of Goddesses
The A to Z Book of Mushrooms
The A to Z Book of Turtle Island
The A to Z Book of Weeds
The A to Z Book of Wildflowers

Also Check out his Other Books

Corpus
Alga and Kevin
Be Not Deceived
Magic Faces – Caras Magicas
Entradas Mexican Doors

Reviews: If you enjoyed this book, Michael P. Earney would appreciate it if you would leave a review on Amazon, Goodreads, or any other Review site you like.

Also, don't forget to tell your friends! Word of mouth advertising is the most precious ***"Thank You"*** a reader can ever give an author.

www.ingramcontent.com/pod-product-compliance
Lightning Source LLC
LaVergne TN
LVHW052357100826
845147LV00013B/865

* 9 7 8 1 9 5 6 5 8 1 2 0 1 *